INTRODUCTION MICROSOFT ONEDRIVE

"Unlocking Seamless Collaboration: A Comprehensive Guide to Maximizing Productivity with Microsoft OneDrive"

BY

ERNEST TWAIN

Table of Contents

INTRODUCTION MICROSOFT ONEDRIVE

Microsoft OneDrive is put away in type of a cloud which can be gotten to with any gadget that contains it. It improves the simple stockpiling of records, reports absent a lot of pressure. Microsoft Onedrive helps you to keep the legitimate plan of records, and the capacity to get to your significant reports, photographs, and some other related documents from an alternate gadget. It likewise accomplishes a lot of work on the best way to share those records or photographs with companions, family, and co-administrators. Microsoft OneDrive can be open on your PC, site, and your cell phone. It likewise aids the appropriate refreshing of each and every document on your PC. Any reports that is been altered or included OneDrive will be synchronized through the cloud to individuals or gadgets you have imparted to already.

Microsoft OneDrive has turned into an extremely fascinating capacity organizer as a result of its simple openness. A most intriguing aspect concerning onedrive is the capacity to open it with a cell phone which makes it simple for everybody to utilize it on the grounds that not every person can bear to get a PC. Regardless of whether you have the envelope on your PC or the application on your cell phone, you can get to it through direct web by composing Onedrive.com and it additionally plays out a similar activity as the one on PC and portable application.

Something else that is extremely significant this is to know the way you can add the document into OneDrive. Furthermore, is exceptionally basic, this is done when you have introduced the application, then, at that point, you find the OneDrive organizer on your PC, after then you simplified the document in the envelope. On account of a cell phone, you can add documents utilizing the OneDrive application. You will turn on camera transfer for you to save each photograph and video taken, and it will work with speedy and simple perspectives on the documents on different gadgets.

Something significant you will comprehend is the way to share records and makes reports on Microsoft onedrive without stress. Sharing of records by means of onedrive tackles the issues of sending monstrous documents through messages. At the point when you share with onedrive they will get the connection to the envelope or records. You ought to likewise remember that all that you on Microsoft onedrive is just seen by you, aside from you, share it with loved ones. With onedrive, you can likewise make Word records like OneNote scratch pad, PowerPoint introductions, and Succeed accounting sheets from any gadget by means of onedrive sites. You simply sign in and select "New" the words record you need to make will appear, then you click on it. There are a lot more things you will find out about Microsoft onedrive as we continue to the accompanying sections.

CHAPTER 1

THE PRIMARY BASIC OF MICROSOFT ONEDRIVE

HOW TO SIGN UP FOR MICROSOFT ONEDRIVE

There are methods you follow while pursuing Microsoft onedrive.

Stage one: Enter the site onedrive.live.com the connection point underneath will be shown and you select "sign up for free"

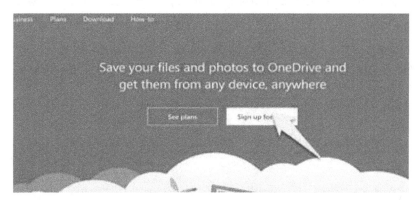

Step two: Choose the account type;

For this situation, you will choose whether to make an individual account or a business account. However, concerning business accounts the elements there are not free of charge.

Sign up

OneDrive	OneDrive for Busin(
Create a Microsoft account	See plans and pricing
If you use Outlook.com or Xbox Live, you already have a Microsoft account.	If your organisation uses Office 3 your work or school account to

Step three: You have to key in your **Email address;**

Space is given to enter your email address, and on the off chance that you don't have a room is given to make one to yourself.

Step four: Enter a new **password;**

After you key in your secret key (password), you click on "next" for the following move to make.

Create a password

Enter the password you would like to use with your account.

Create password

☐ Show password

enter password

Next

Step five: Other details

At this level, you are expected to demonstrate your nation and your date of birth.

Create account

We need just a little more info to set up your account.

Country/region

Nigeria

Date of birth

Day ⌄ Month ⌄ Year ⌄

Next

Step six: Verification of your email address;

After this multitude of cycles a code will be shipped off your telephone number or email for legitimate affirmation to guarantee you are the proprietor of the email or telephone number. Then you will type in the code for it to be affirmed.

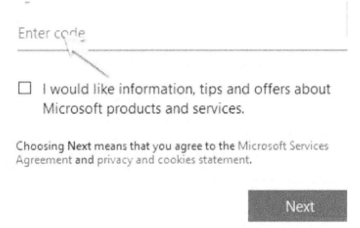

Enter code

☐ I would like information, tips and offers about Microsoft products and services.

Choosing Next means that you agree to the Microsoft Services Agreement and privacy and cookies statement.

Next

Step seven: Final confirmation and account creation;

At this stage, you need to demonstrate you are human by entering the manual human test code accurately, after then your record has been made and you can now transfer your documents and archives to your account.

Create account

Before proceeding, we need to make sure that a real person is creating this account.

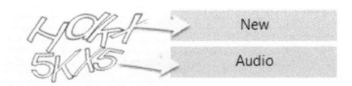

New

Audio

Enter the characters you see

ONEDRIVE ON YOUR COMPUTER

The tool you are utilizing decides the way in which you will get onedrive on your framework. On account of a PC, the windows you are utilizing are placed into thought, for instance, in the event that you are utilizing Windows

7 you really want to Download OneDrive, with respect to my PC is window 10 as of now contains onedrive. Simply click on onedrive and adhere to the guidance to introduce the application.

Set up OneDrive

Put your files in OneDrive to get them from any device.

Enter your email address

Create account   Sign in

1.   Open and adhered to the guidance to "introduced" the application.

Click on begin and follow the orders.

Clicking "Get started" means you agree to the Microsoft service agreement and privacy statement. OneDrive may also download and install its updates automatically.

Get started

2.   At the point when you have effectively introduced the onedrive on your PC. Onedrive envelope will be added consequently to Windows Explorer.

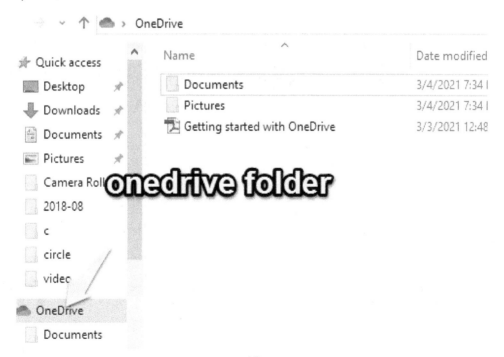

OPENING ONEDRIVE ONLINE AND COMPLETING FUNDAMENTAL TASK

HOW TO CREATE FOLDER AND OTHER DOCUMENTS IN ONEDRIVE

Here, we will guide you on the best way to make organizers and other related record in onedrive absent a lot of pressure. Onedrive has made it simple for you to get to any of your records or documents regardless of where you are. We will initially frame the move toward make an envelope in onedrive.

HOW TO CREATE A FOLDER

Coming up next are steps and techniques to make an envelope in onedrive.

1.   You will tap on "new" then, at that point, you p " from the down-drop menu.

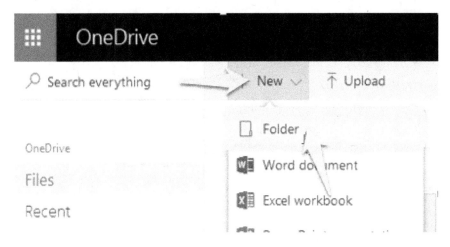

2.   You will type the name of the folder and tap on **create** to continue.

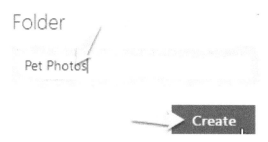

3. After the above method, your envelope will be made, then you will tap on the organizer to get to it. The screen underneath will show.

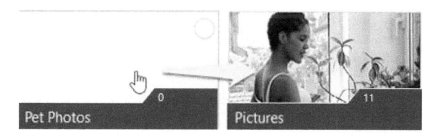

HOW TO CREATE A DOCUMENT

For this situation, you likewise follow a similar system use in making an organizer.

1. You click on the new handle, then you enter the ideal record you need to make starting from the drop menu.

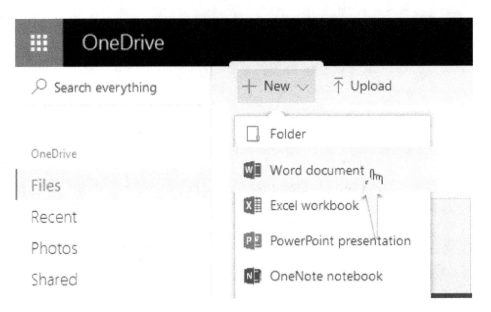

2. After which your report will be made and simultaneously opened without a moment's delay. The following is a run of the mill illustration of a word report interface show in Microsoft onedrive.

HOW TO SEARCH FOR FILE AND SAVED IN ONEDRIVE CLOUD

In the event that you mind your onedrive storage on the web it contains a hunt all that case situated at the upper right flank. Click in the case, then you enter the name of the document you are looking for, and accessible ideas will be made so that you might see whether that is the thing you are looking for. You can tap on any of the proposed results assuming you found what you were looking for or you click on to see more outcomes to see the total rundown.

Onedrive enjoys a few different benefits while looking for records and reports. Onedrive additionally look through on filenames and inside the report, as PDFs, Word records, and PowerPoint show documents. Right now, you can likewise restrict the proposed outcome that will be shown via looking through the records type and date drop-down menu at the top. This assists in lessening with focusing on while looking for a specific record or report in Microsoft onedrive. For instance, I need to see photographs of the most recent fourteen days, utilizing the sort and date drop-down menu will be of good assistance to you.

Another significant thing is to save what you look for, so you can get to it next time absent a lot of pressure. The screen capture show beneath demonstrates a saved hunt menu where you save your records. There is likewise a nearby inquiry which will assist you with finishing your quest for any files or documents.

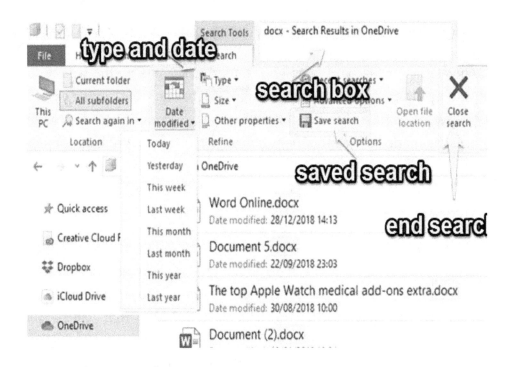

HOW TO UPLOAD FILES IN ONEDRIVE

Certain individuals imagine that onedrive is just for putting away records or archives, yet it isn't the case. Microsoft onedrive can likewise be utilized to transfer documents like photographs, music, and recordings, and so on. Under this sub-heading, we will make sense of exhaustively how for utilize your PC to transfer records or reports in onedrive absent a lot of pressure. Follow the technique underneath to make it happen.

1. The Principal thing you ought to do is to find the record you wish to transfer on your PC. From the screen capture underneath I show the document I need to transfer.

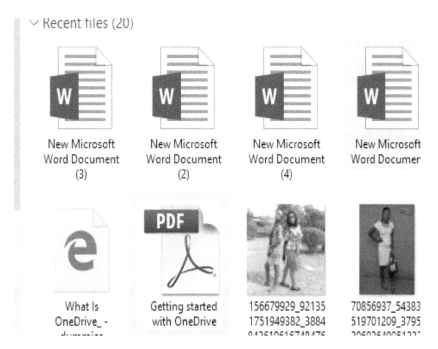

2. Then you will click on the **file** you want to upload and drag it to onedrive folders.

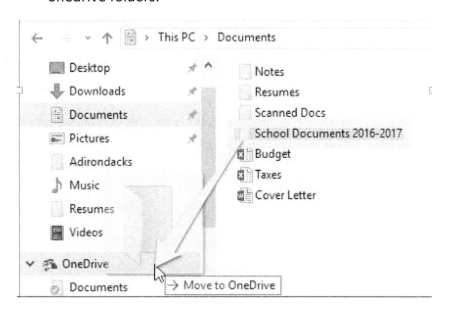

3. After then you will see your record appearing on the onedrive.

HOW TO UPLOAD FILES ON THE WEB IN ONEDRIVE

In a circumstance where you don't approach onedrive PC application, transferring through the web will be another option. With a web uploader, you can transfer your documents on the net absent a lot of battle. However, contrasting with the PC application it is a piece slow and tedious and is likewise a simple methodology to transfer your records or reports anyplace you track down yourself. The move toward continue in document transferring on the web are expressed beneath.

1.   Move to onedrive. Then, at that point, you find and pick the transfer button.

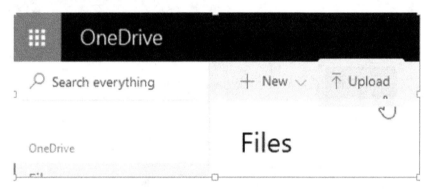

2.   You need to find and pick the document you need to transfer. You can transfer various records as you wish essentially by choosing and holding down the Ctrl key, then snap to open.

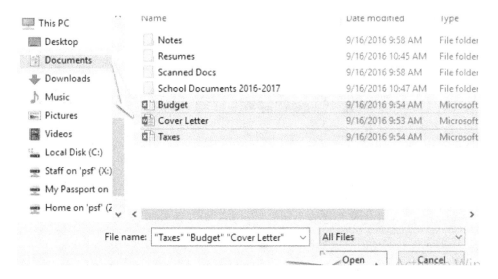

3.	After a couple of cycles up until this point your record will be shipped off your onedrive.

CHAPTER TWO

THE ONEDRIVE INTERFACE

EXPLORING THE ONEDRIVE INTERFACE

The onedrive connection point envelops the rundown of all you ought to be aware of Microsoft onedrive. It gives an outline of what onedrive is about. It has to do with the major idea of onedrive. Under this subject, we will brief five things you ought to know fundamentally about Microsoft onedrive. The main thing is to realize what is implied by onedrive.

1.   DEFINITION OF ONEDRIVE

Onedrive could be characterized as a web-based Microsoft cloud that stores records and reports on its foundation. Onedrive was first known as SkyDrive, yet later run it was rebrand before in 2014 because of a brand name issue raised by Joined Realm neighborhood telecaster. Onedrive absorbed into window 10 and furthermore as an application on Android telephone, Windows telephone, iOS, and on the web through any internet browser. On this stage, administrators can store their photographs, recordings, music, and other significant reports.

2.   HOW YOU CAN ACCESS ONEDRIVE

You might have perceived numerous ideas around onedrive yet we will examine with you the major idea connected with onedrive in a concise organization. Here you will figure out how to sign in and out onedrive.

The most effective method to SIGN IN MICROSOFT ONEDRIVE (for Window 10)

For you to utilize onedrive on your PC, you need to sign in to your record. You need to follow the strategy beneath for you to sign in onedrive records.

Step 1. **Double tap** on the Microsoft onedrive symbol on your PC.

Step 2. The screen underneath will show then you click on sign in to get to your record.

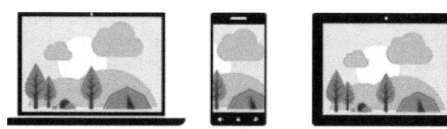

Step 3. The framework will demand you to enter in your subtleties for your Microsoft or onedrive record. After then, you will tap on the sign-in button.

Sign in

Microsoft account What's this?

Password

Sign in

Step 4. . After then you will be shown the succeeding screen, you will tap the Following handle to utilize the defaulting area with the goal that the onedrive envelope will be saved, on the other hand you can likewise pick an area for your OneDrive organizer simply by tapping on Change area interface and a new area is picking.

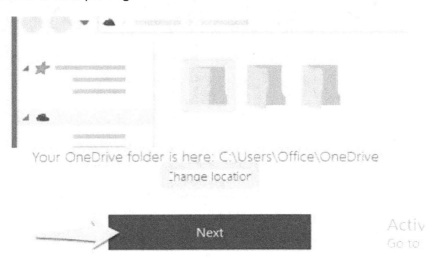

Your OneDrive folder is here: C:\Users\Office\OneDrive
Change location

Next

Activ
Go to

Step 5. This is the keep going move toward take, on your PC, you are expected to pick the envelope that you wish to adjust your onedrive organizer. The one tick is chosen to adjust to the organizer.

After which, you click on the following button to continue to arrangement. Then, at that point, you can now tap on the handle.

☑ Sync all files and folders in my OneDrive

Sync only these folders

☑ ☐ Files not in a folder (182.9 KB)

> ☑ ▮ Air Doc (36.0 KB)

> ☑ ▮ Documents (0.1 KB)

> ☑ ▮ Favorites (0.0 KB)

> ☑ ▮ New folder (0.0 KB)

> ☑ ▮ Pictures (0.0 KB)

> ☑ ▮ Public (0.0 KB)

> ☑ ▮ Screenshots (770.0 KB)

Selected: 989.0 KB

Remaining space on C: 366.9 GB

Next

Sign out from OneDrive (for Windows 10)

We should expect you need to erase OneDrive, you simply need to sign out of your Microsoft OneDrive record, and the OneDrive envelope will be erased mechanically from your PC. You have to the means/methodology underneath to sign out your OneDrive record with less pressure.

Step 1. Right-click on the Microsoft OneDrive symbol that will be situated in your PC locale of the taskbar, and you will be expected to click Settings for you to get to Microsoft OneDrive settings.

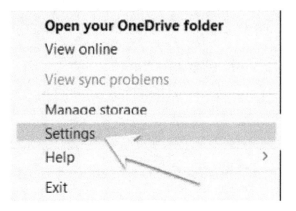

Step 2. At present, you want to move to the Records tab by tapping or tapping on the Records tag.

Step 3. You will be expected to tap the button marked as "UnlinkOneDrive" control.

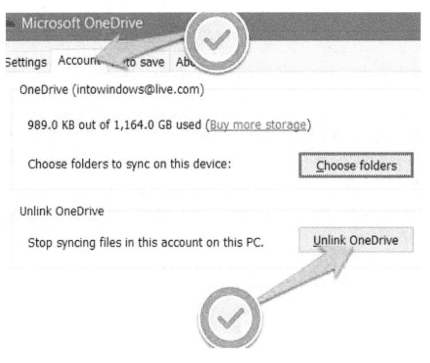

Step 4. At the point when the record is successfully unlinked, you will see the "Welcome to OneDrive" show with the "Sign in" charge.

Welcome to OneDrive

Put your files in OneDrive to get to them from any device.

Sign in with your Microsoft account.

Sign in

3.   HOW Install folders/files

The least difficult endeavor on OneDrive is to parcel a Record or Envelope. You need to follow the methodology that are given underneath to share an OneDrive document or Envelope. Access the web, right-click on a document to get a connection you will use to share the record. You need to send the connection by means of your email record, or offer straight on Facebook (this can be conceivable assuming that your virtual entertainment network is connected to your Microsoft onedrive record).

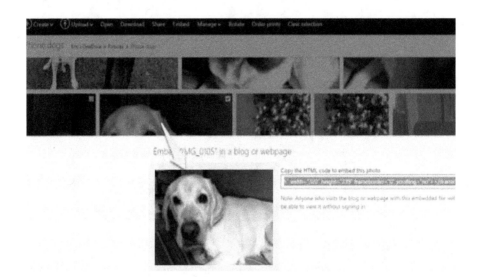

Implanting could be characterized as the most common way of showing something exhaustively, for moments, the screen capture above gives a run of the mill illustration of an installed picture. A few cycles can be utilized in implanting a YouTube video on a web page. For this to be finished in a simple and basic structure you need to apply the implanted order, this install order will assist in creating a HTML with coding, which can be utilized on a blogger or web page.

4.   The most effective method to SAVE ALL OFFICE Documents TO ONEDRIVE

The OneDrive and Microsoft Office programs are very associated. For you to utilize OneDrive as your default, you need to save area, then, at that point, you will trail the unassuming advances given to you beneath.

The main thing you need to do is to sign in to your OneDrive record. The explanation while we are utilizing MS Office is that you can rapidly bungle regardless of whether you are endorsed in by any unobtrusive strategy.

After you sign in, while attempting to save a new record, the significant elective that will be perceptible is OneDrive. At the point when you click Peruse and you will procure a rundown that will show the nearby OneDrive organizers on your hard drive. You are expected to tap the Pin symbol close to any envelope and it will continuously be saved as the avoidance area helping with saving each Office archives.

5.   The most effective method to GET Extra SPACE IN MICROSOFT ONEDRIVE

OneDrive offers 5GB of free space for capacity. On the other hand, on the off chance that you have been utilizing OneDrive for quite a while you can guarantee 15 or 25GB of free space for capacity. Concerning the reports, there are restricted means by which you can include extra free space your OneDrive record for capacity. For instance now, assuming that you share this assistance with the vast majority of your companions, you can acquire extra 10GB of free stockpiling. You can save records or archives of any kind, up until this point they are not higher than 10GB per document. However, assuming that you actually need more space, OneDrive will offer you some capacity plans which can be reasonable for you.

SETTING UP YOUR MICROSOFT ONEDRIVE ACCOUNT

To set up Microsoft OneDrive is exceptionally basic for those of you utilizing Windows 10 it is more straightforward in light of the fact that there is no requirement for you to download the application for establishment. All you really want to do is to check the application and proceed with the other set-up strategies. For you to know how simple Microsoft OneDrive is with Window 10, during the Window 10 arrangement you will be found out if you will jump at the chance to utilize OneDrive assuming that you couldn't acknowledge OneDrive it will in any case be realistic for you on the framework. In a circumstance where the symbol won't come up, then, at that point, you should provoke from OneDrive exe document. However, for any of us utilizing a less redesigned Windows, you will be expected to download the application from the application store.

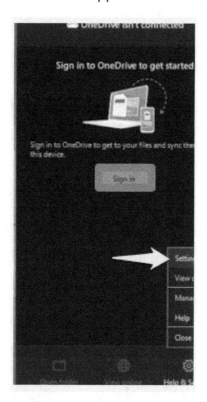

In the organizer, you will double tap on the OneDrive.exe record, and the picture will show in the PC plate. Then you need to right-tap on the representation and pick Settings. You need to tap on the Settings tab and you ought to guarantee that the case to Begin OneDrive mechanically when you begin marking in to Windows is confound.

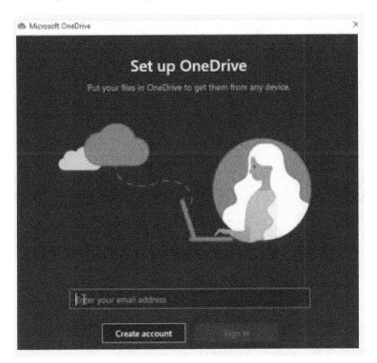

On the Settings screen recently displayed to you, then, at that point, click the Record tab and pick the Add a record control. On the Set-up OneDrive showcase, you will to enter in the email address for your Microsoft Record and from that point forward, you click on Sign in. You need to choose your sort of Microsoft OneDrive record, whether is for Work, School, or Individual. Key in your secret phrase and snap on Sign in. You will be expected to approve the place that Microsoft has previously set on your OneDrive envelope. You might choose to substitute the position or you concede the default and snap on Straightaway.

HOW TO ADD FILE MICROSOFT ONEDRIVE

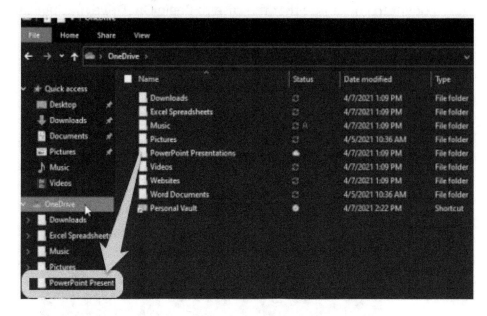

What you are expected to do next is to pick the organizers and records you need to add and synchronize to the OneDrive stashing. From your Document Pioneer, you can choose to move records and organizers of your decision to match up them into where your OneDrive is found. For example, on the off chance that you choose to utilize an organizer like PowerPoint Present for your Microsoft documents, you will move the entire envelope into Microsoft OneDrive (the cluster strategy would be in the accompanying organizations C:\Users\[username]\OneDrive\ PowerPoint present).

THE CLOUD STORAGE

There is a requirement for you to choose to save your matched up documents or you will likewise be given a choice to download your synchronized records when you want them. Simply click on the Settings tab and you want to look through on the setting and select Documents On-Request, which you will empower naturally. With the assistance of this setting when you turn it on, your Microsoft OneDrive will be saved online instead of on your PC.

The relations to your documents which are online consistently show in your record traveler. On the off chance that you click a record two times to open it, the document is as of now downloaded as it moves from OneDrive to your PC. The beneficial thing about Documents On-Request is the way that more space is been kept on your hard drive. There is one major disservice is that you are expected to open your record just when you are on the web.

You can choose to forsake this specific other option in the event that you have various spaces in your hard drive yet you can enact it when negligible extra room. In some situation,s you can simply all alone choose to store a few sure records and organizers on the web and the rest both physically and on the web. You really want to tap on the checkbox to switch off this other option.

HOW TO BACK UP FILES WITH ONEDRIVE

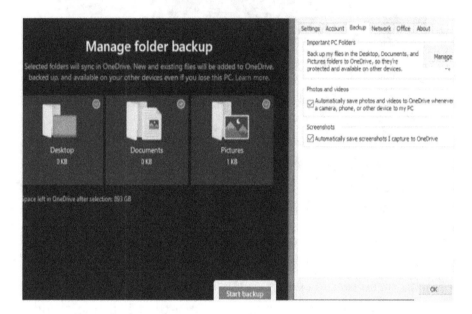

Presently, you have been working with OneDrive constantly. You have done such countless things ready around OneDrive, it can likewise be utilized to recuperate exceptionally important records or envelopes. Most importantly, you will enter the OneDrive program window, you click on a tab that demonstrates reinforcement after then pick Oversee reinforcement. You can choose to back up the work area, pictures, and reports envelope. You need to choose the things you need a reinforcement, after wish you click on a tab name Start reinforcement.

HOW TO CREATE A PHOTO ALBUM IN ONEDRIVE

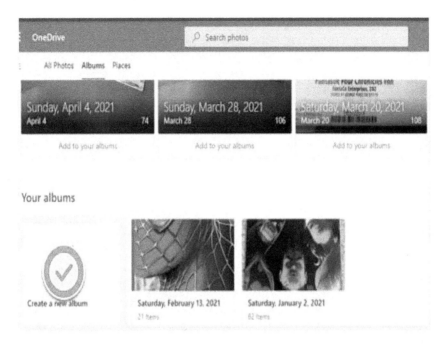

In the first place, we realize that collections are an assortment of records or reports like pictures, music, recordings, etc in mass. You can make your photograph or video collections basically by picking those photographs or recordings that is been saved in your OneDrive record. On that OneDrive site where your record is sign in, you will tap the Section for those photos at the left board. You need to tap on the subtitle for Collections, then, at that point, click on Make another collection button at the main thumbnail. Give the suitable title you like to your collection, pick those photos you like to add, after that you click on Add Collection and you have effectively make a Collection.

HOW TO TURN OFF AUTOMATIC SYNC IN ONEDRIVE

Presently, you might have chosen to release your PC from your OneDrive record, first thing need to do is to guarantee that each record you need were synchronized to that specific PC. This should be possible by means of getting to the OneDrive plate symbols. You will pick Settings > Record > select organizers. You need to really look at the crate to Match up each record and envelope in OneDrive, in a circumstance where you had uncontrolled any documents or envelopes previously.

The activity we have done as such far will consequently download a few documents from the OneDrive record which has not been in presence on your PC. The methodology will take a long while, yet we can likewise look at the achievement by means of right-tapping the OneDrive Situation plate symbol to see how far and time is left on it.

Up to this point all of your records is supported as of now to your PC, you will right-tap on the OneDrive Situation plate symbol and pick Settings. On that Settings tab, you uncheck the container to Begin OneDrive mechanically assuming you sign in to Windows. Then, at that point, you need to tap the

Record tab and snap the Unlink the PC association. On exceptionally fast notification, you click on the Unlink account button, and after this, your framework will no more match up with your OneDrive account.

CHAPTER 3

SIGNING IN TO MICROSOFT ONEDRIVE

We have examined momentarily how to sign in to Microsoft OneDrive in the past part under the Microsoft OneDrive connection point, yet presently we will regard it exhaustively as a subject all alone. Here we will likewise underscore things you want to do before you can sign in for OneDrive.

There are two different ways you can sign in to OneDrive, either through the site page or with the application. In the event that you as of now have the application on your framework, you will sign in with the accompanying systems beneath. Yet, in a circumstance where you don't have the application on your framework, then, at that point, you will either introduce the application or sign in through the website page (onedrive.live.com).

1.   You will tap on the Beginning pursuit case and type "OneDrive." Then you will see OneDrive appearance in the hunt results, then, at that point, click on it.

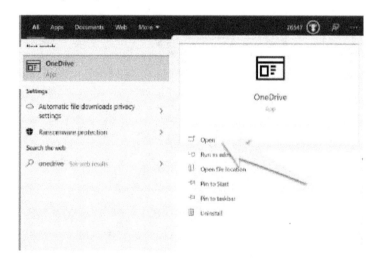

2.   At the point when you as of now have a record with OneDrive, you will simply enter the email address you utilized in pursuing the record, then, at that point, you will tap on "sign in."

Put your files in OneDrive to get them from any device.

Enter your email address

3. After that you enter your secret key on the following page. In the event that you have previously set up a couple of things verification for your Microsoft account, you will be expected to enter an extra code shipped off your email or telephone number for legitimate affirmation of record possession.

4. You need to trail the orders to choose the OneDrive envelope you need. On the off chance that you have endorsed in before on this framework, you might have a predominant OneDrive organizer. You can snap to utilize that envelope or you will choose another one.

A OneDrive folder already exists on this PC

If you're connecting with the same OneDrive account as before, choose "U... , choose a new location to avoid ...g files from two accounts

old | Use this folder

new | Choose new folder

HOW TO MANAGE YOUR ONEDRIVE FOLDERS

You can likewise do various exercises and play out a few exercises for a specific record or envelope in your Microsoft OneDrive record with the guide of the "Manage" elective. You, most importantly, need to pick an envelope or document and after that activity, you will tap on the "Manage" elective start at the top, and the reachable option is displayed to you at the down-drop menus which contain "Rename", "Erase", "Move to", "Duplicate to", "Form History" and "Properties". The option of seeing the envelope or document's that you rolled out a new improvement on before is made conceivable through the rendition history and furthermore the property segment gives you subtleties data concerning the thing you have picked. Underneath will give subtleties of a portion of the symbols featured in striking structure.

HOW TO SORT OUT YOUR FILES

Assuming you move to the OneDrive key page, you will see each document and envelope on the principal page. You will choose the documents to see by simply picking a few options in the left triangulation board.

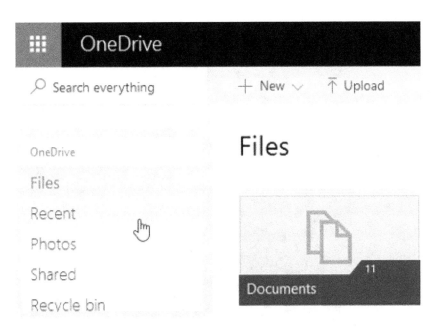

You can also alternate how your file should be displayed via clicking the **Outlook Alternatives** icon at the top right corner.

There are a few strategies you can use in survey documents on Microsoft OneDrive. The underneath are ways you can see documents on OneDrive with illustrative models.

1. Photograph Viewpoint: This is one of the most mind-blowing ways of review your record or envelope particularly when you have a specific envelope of photographs that you really do go through at spans. It provides you with an outline of thumbnails of your photographs moved down in the network.

2.   List Standpoint: It grants you to see your documents with the names related with them and other vital data, that you might be acquainted with assuming you typically work with those organizers and records on your PC.

Files

	↑ Name	Date modified	Sharing	Size
	Documents	11/1/2012		1.59 MB
	Music	5/8/2014		358 KB
	Pet Photos	8:51 AM		
	Pictures	11/1/2012		4.85 MB
	Public	11/1/2012	⌀ Owner	
	BdayInvites.docx	9/16/2016	⌀ Owner	13.6 KB
	Book1.xlsx	10/24/2016	⌀ Owner	7.45 KB
	Cover Letter.docx	9/16/2016		13.6 KB

3.   Tiles Viewpoint: it permits you to locate your documents and organizers in a matrix of symbols. This kind of view is an avoidance view for your envelopes and documents.

Files

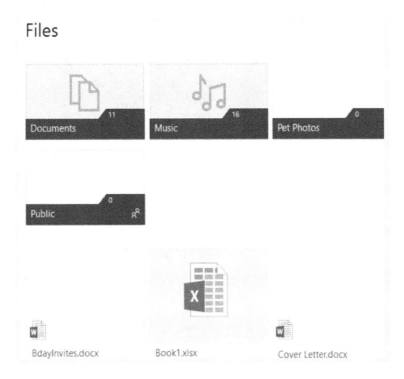

Documents   11

Music   16

Pet Photos   0

Public   0

BdayInvites.docx

Book1.xlsx

Cover Letter.docx

SEARCHING FOR YOUR FILES

You can look for archives by means of the inquiry article. Looking for your reports, license you to look for an exact record utilizing words which are restricted inside the report and its name.

•   To look for a record, you will tap on the inquiry bar. Enter the words or title you wish to look for after then click Enter. What you were looking for will show.

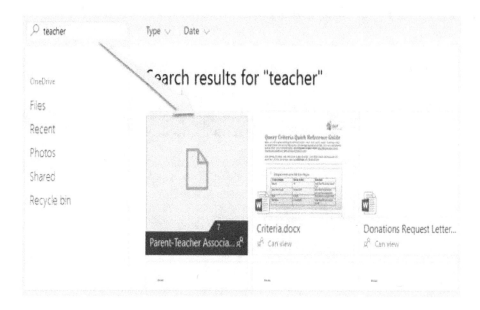

WORKING WITH YOUR FOLDERS

Your envelope can be utilized in putting together your documents. You can store your reports in an envelope and you can likewise move a record from one organizer to the next without stress. The part of moving reports between various envelopes is entirely reasonable in light of the fact that the record can be shared by simply moving the record to a Common Organizer. For example, we should expect you are working on a specific task with some arrangement of people, you might choose to impart your organizer to them. From that point forward, you will settle on the record you wish to impart to the arrangement of the person to the common envelope.

HOW YOU CAN MOVE A FILE TO A FOLDER

1. Float the mouse over any document, then, at that point, click on the really look at box at the upper right flank. You can choose to pick various documents essentially by clicking extra actually look at boxes.

Shared > Parent-Teacher Association Fundraising

2.   Tap on the **Move to** control in the menu at the top-right flank.

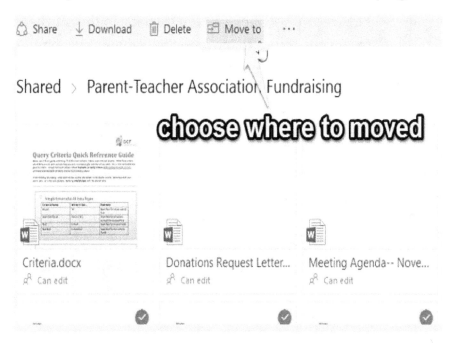

3.   The Move objects to the board will show on the right flank of the screen. Pick the organizer where you will get a kick out of the chance to move the record to after you click on Move.

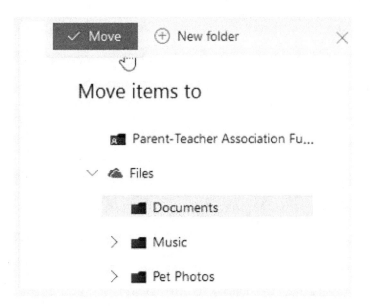

4. Your record will move as you train it. On the off chance that you favor your record to move to the common organizer, it will do so and will likewise be imparted to a gathering and companions.

OTHER FILE ALTERNATIVES

If you have any desire to get additional record overseeing choices, you will be expected to right-tap on that document. The screen capture underneath shows a commonplace illustration of additional choices given to you.

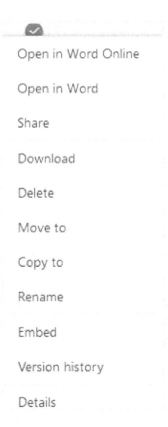

Open in Word Online

Open in Word

Share

Download

Delete

Move to

Copy to

Rename

Embed

Version history

Details

A large portion of these choices incorporate the accompanying:

• Rendition history: Open and restore recently put away variants of the records.

• Download: It is an approach to saving a duplicate of the document to your PC. The report which you download before won't be updated when changes are been made to them in Microsoft OneDrive.

• Rename: Here you will substitute the name of the records.

• Erase: at the point when you erase any document it will move to the Reuse Container naturally. For every one of the documents to be at last erased you are expected to exhaust the reuse receptacle.

HOW TO EXPLORE OTHER ALTERNATIVES ON ONEDRIVE WEBSITE

The presentation of Microsoft has made it exceptionally simple for you to keep appropriate creation of different contenders and furthermore, in the part of distributed storage, Microsoft foundation has additionally pushed their image which was recently known as SkyDrive yet as of now, the name of the new brand has been changing to OneDrive. In contrast with another cloud administration, Microsoft's OneDrive offers their administrators a free 7GB extra room and you will likewise be given an extra putting away space when you choose to make a Microsoft account. In this slide, we clear up for you exhaustively many highlights and devices which will be seen on the OneDrive site simply register for OneDrive and get your Record prepared, then track the method that will be displayed to you underneath.

HOW YOU CAN ACCESS ONEDRIVE Site

For you to open the OneDrive site this can happen regularly as you frequently access numerous different sites. All you really want to do is to get to your favored program and once is available you will just enter "onedrive.live.com" into the web address search box and snap "Enter" on your framework console. When have effectively access the OneDrive site, a connection point will show where you will be expected to enter in your email and secret key you utilized in making your Microsoft account into the spaces accommodated that data and you will be immediate to the principal page of your OneDrive record. There are various techniques to follow to reach out to the OneDrive site.

Presently, assuming you look on the principal page of the OneDrive record, you will be shown dull blue thumbnails at the highest point of the screen which addresses a few organizers that you can store transferred documents into. On the off chance that you put your mouse pointer on any of those envelopes you will see a little square box at the upper right-flank of the thumbnail. Assuming you choose to click inside the little square box, you will see an obvious sign that will show in that container. This check displayed on the square box demonstrate that those things have been picked. At the top segment of the screen beneath, any remaining options for the picked thing are shown.

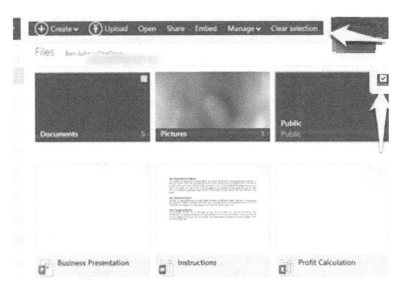

HOW TO CREATE DISSIMILAR FILES USING OFFICE ONLINE

Assuming you mind the OneDrive site's principal page, there is space for you to make different sorts of records or archives like Succeed, PowerPoint, and Word, every one of these should be possible without any Microsoft OfficeSuite on your PC work area screen. By and by, it's extremely simple for you to chip away at documents of any sort keenly in the mean time you are in any Microsoft's web-based administrations like OneDrive and this can be exceptionally straightforward with the guide of "Office On the web" applications. For you to play out this activity made sense of for you, simply click on the "Make" button that is the site at the top flank of the screen and when you are finished doing as such, then the applications that will help you in making the record will be displayed to you at the drop-down menu, click on it to get a new document

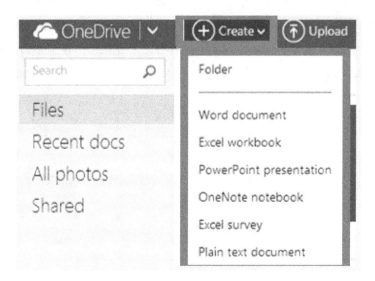

HOW TO OPEN A FILE IN DESKTOP OR ONLINE OFFICE APP

On the off chance that you as of now have a few records put away in your OneDrive record, you can investigate the choices by they way you can open any of them. The most lovely part OneDrive is the way that it very well may be acclimatized with your Windows framework regardless of the internet browser you generally use in marking in to your OneDrive record. Presently we should investigate the methodology to embrace to get to a record. We have two strategies to play out this activity. You can get to and alter your record on a few Internet based Office applications or play out a comparable work on each application's work area relating to the part of the Microsoft Office assortment. Simply pick a record taking on the techniques that we have given to you beforehand and when you are finished picking, then, at that point, you will be savvy to see an option at the top flank designated "Open". At the point when you are finished tapping on this other option and you will permit to see two possible determinations while getting to the file.

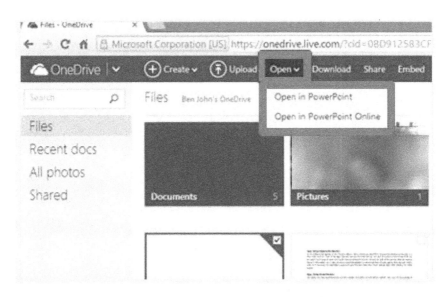

The "Open" options on the screen above demonstrate both "PowerPoint" and "PowerPoint On the web" however we have picked a PowerPoint document from our Microsoft OneDrive record.

HOW TO DOWNLOAD A FILE OR FOLDER TO YOUR COMPUTER OR MOBILE DEVICE

One elective which will regularly show at the top segment of the Microsoft OneDrive significant page when you click on any record is the "Download" elective. This option can likewise be utilized to get anything you have created before with your cell phone and saved it in OneDrive, you can choose to duplicate those things to a PC hard drive. For you to any happy in OneDrive, you are expected to pick the record or whatever other report that is been saved money on your PC hard drive, after then click on the Download elective at the top segment of the page.

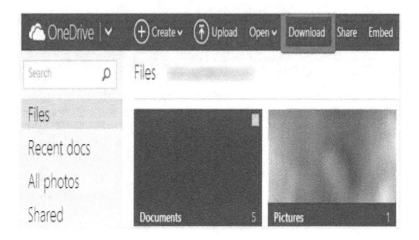

HOW TO SHARE A FILE OR FOLDER, OTHER PEOPLE

There is another elective that pulled in me definitely, how to impart my record to others without stress. What's more, this specific option is just realistic on the OneDrive site page which is shown share. The reason for the order is now shown with the name, it licenses you to share any envelope or record for anyone that is on your rundown of contact so they will actually want to download or see the document.   This is an uncommon strategy to help out your companions on your virtual entertainment like Facebook, Twitter, Instagram, and so on. The "Offer" elective warrants you to be associated towards a specific record that you have featured and send the document to any of your companions either by messaging or as a message through visit. Consequently reward message will be added and you can likewise substitute the manner in which your recipients can chip away at those documents.

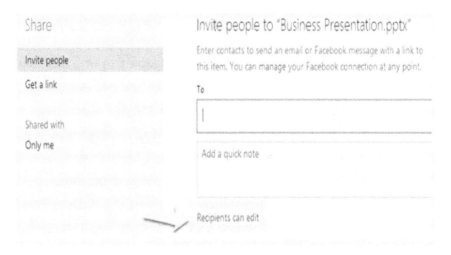

On the off chance that you view the screen capture above you will see a connection designate "Recipient can alter" and on the off chance that you click on it, it will show to both of you drop-down options that will empower you to choose whether the document recipient ought to have the option to alter or see the record just and furthermore demonstrate whether the record collector should sign in their Microsoft account before they can concede the grant to see the record. At the point when you are through with this record readiness, contributing the collector name then click on the Offer button situated at the base flank of the screen.

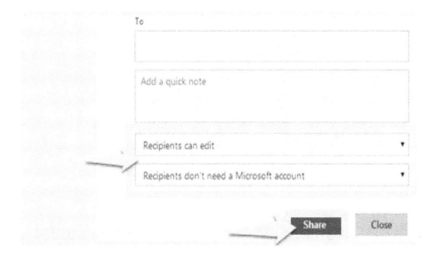

HOW TO EMBED A FILE TO YOUR BLOG OR WEB PAGE

In certain circumstances, you will likewise get a site or a blog where you will like to move your record in. In the event that you believe this should happen you need to deliver a HTML code easily for any document utilizing this elective which designates "Implant" which is situated at the top segment when you access your OneDrive by means of the web. You click on the button which shows Insert subsequent to tapping on the button, a mail will ship off you as screen convergence that gives subtleties of what leave or enter, all you want to do is to tap on the "Create" button for you to get the HTML code which will be ship off you for you to place envelope or record into any of your blog or website page and you will actually want to share to various people visiting your page at a time.

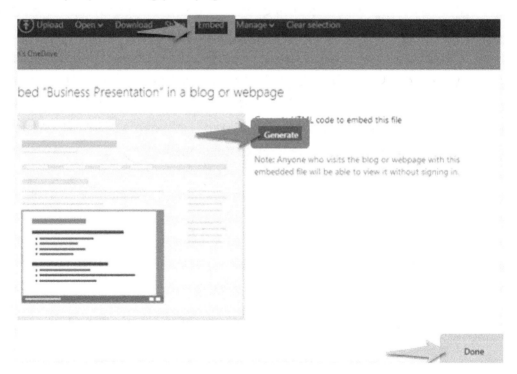

TOOLS USE FOR SHARING IN MICROSOFT ONEDRIVE

Presently you have prevailed with regards to offering a record or report to others, the report or record you have imparted to them will approach the record whenever they wish. At times, assuming that you award them the option to modify any adjustment of the record or report, they will can do as such with the workplace online absent a lot of pressure. Something significant about it is that few individuals can alter a specific common record or document at an at once. Assuming there is any requirement for you to see somebody altering a similar common record with you, you will actually want to see the individual at the upper right flank of the page. From the screen capture show to you beneath, the name of the individual altering a similar common record is JULIA FILLORY.

In however much somebody substitute a specific report you approach previously, you will can see the place of their different cursor, another you ought to know is that you won't have the admittance to see their alter until they save their variation. The rotation that have been done as such far will material to each release of the archives.

Reality with regards to it is that you can't foresee this strategy for sharing the record. In a circumstance where are altering at the same time with others, the variation made on the report won't show immediately. There is a requirement for you to revive or return the report before you will actually want to see its current alters.

You likewise need to discuss the common reports essentially by adding what we called archive remarks. In the event that you remark on any report you have shared before with various individuals, it will be extremely simple for them to view and answer to any remark you have made on the record.

• For you to have the option to include to remark the record, you need to visit OneDrive, then, at that point, guarantee that the data board is additionally detectible, and pick the specific report you need to remark on. The last thing you ought to do is to enter in your remark in the remarks box situated at the base flank of the realities board. After you wrap up composing your remark in the remark box, then, at that point, you click on add to effectively make it. The following is an ordinary illustration of what we are referring to.

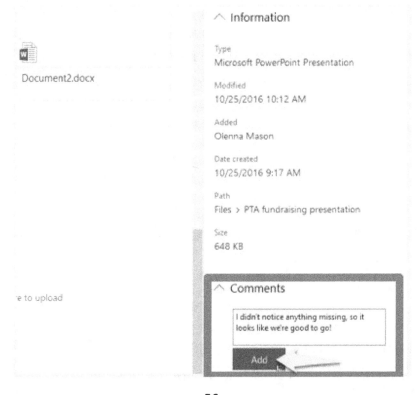

CHAPTER 4

OPEN A DOCUMENT WITH OFFICE ONLINE

A ton of work should be possible on your reports through a web program with the assistance of an internet based office. One of the large benefits that makes Office Online pertinent is that it helps the individuals who don't have the workplace application on their work area to get to it through the web. You can get to and alter every one of the records you have in any web program with Office On the web. However, in a circumstance where you have previously introduced Microsoft Office on your framework, you can simply go on access the application and alter the reports with the work area Office series. One more significant thing when you alter your records with Office Online is the altering instruments, it has more elements and altering devices when contrasted with the Workplace work area application.

HOW TO OPEN A DOCUMENT WITH OFFICE ONLINE

1. What you need to do is to tap on the specific record you need to gain admittance to. In the representation given beneath, we pick a PowerPoint record to give an example.

2. At the point when you see your document it will get to a new tag. At the top toolbar, you are expected to click Alter Show, then, at that point, pick Alter in Program from the down-drop menu show beneath.

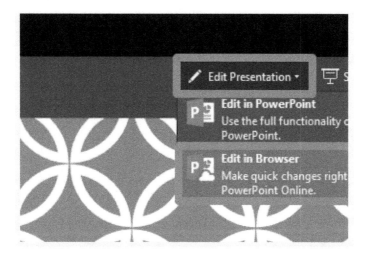

3. Naturally your report will show. You can proceed to do your altering with office online absent a lot of pressure.

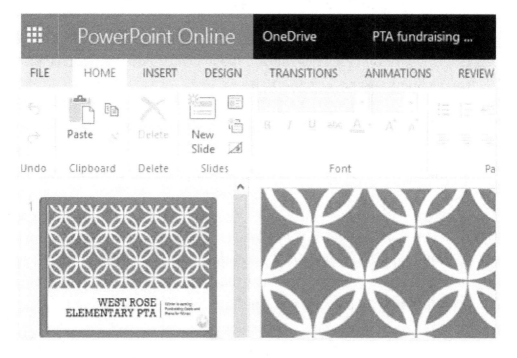

For you to close the record and return to OneDrive, you will tap on the OneDrive association at the highest point of the screen underneath.

HOW TO TURN OFF, DISABLE, OR UNINSTALLED ONEDRIVE

At the point when you have chosen not to utilize OneDrive any longer, all you really want to do is to detach it from your framework. Also, there are methods you will follow for it to be done without a hitch.

Something else is that, assuming you want to quit adjusting records to OneDrive for quite a while, all you really want to do is to stop OneDrive for certain minutes and sync thereafter.

Notes:

•   You ought to remember that you won't lose any records or information during the time spent debilitating OneDrive on your PC. The best way to open your records is through marking in to the site > OneDrive.com.

In Windows 10, OneDrive is the avoidance save an objective for every one of your records and reports. What this infers is that new records or reports are mechanically put away to OneDrive, with the exception of you choose to save to a different objective on your PC.

HOW TO UNLINK ONEDRIVE

1.   What you do, pick the OneDrive cloud symbol sited at the notice segment, at the base right corner of your work area.

Footnote: some time you might be expected to tap on the Show Stowed away Symbol demonstrated by bolt ^ which is towards the warning area before you can have the option to see the OneDrive symbol. In a circumstance where the OneDrive symbol isn't appearing in the notice segment, then you ought to know that OneDrive won't run. You need to pick Start, then, at that point, you type OneDrive in the pursuit region, from the outcomes displayed to you pick OneDrive.

2.   You pick More > Settings

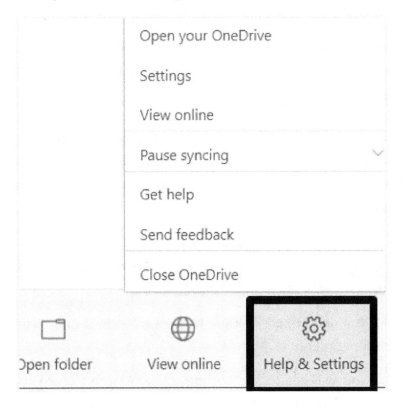

3.   The most effective method to Stow away OneDrive

OneDrive is been made into chosen sorts of Windows and you can't uninstall it. The main thing you can do to it is to conceal the symbol and delay the sync system, it will remain stowed away. For this to be done effectively, you will switch off each OneDrive setting and dispose of the OneDrive envelope from the document traveler.

For Windows 10.

For you to have the option to conceal your OneDrive symbol. There is not a problem about it all you want to do is to follow the above step. Similar technique we follow to unlink OneDrive, additionally equivalent to concealing OneDrive on Windows 10.

1.   The Settings tag, you to uncheck each container which is under the Overall menu.

2.   The AutoSave tag, fixed the Archives and Pictures slants to The PC alone, and you uncheck different boxes from it.

 In the Record tag, you will tap on the envelopes you have picked.

3.   You will Match up your Microsoft OneDrive records to your PC box, you ought to check and uncheck the crate at Sync for each document and envelope on your OneDrive. Then you click the alright button to end the crate and it will return to settings.

The above system we have taken up until this point will dispose of each and every OneDrive record from your PC however will treat with them on the site (OneDrive.lives.com).

4.   You need to click alright to save any adjustments you have made in the Settings menu.

5.   You will get to the Settings over. At the Record tag, you click on Unlink OneDrive. Then you close the Greeting to OneDrive menu that shows.

6.   You will get to the Record Adventurer, you right-click on OneDrive, and afterward you click on Properties.

On the off chance that you investigate the General tag, towards the Qualities, you jumble the Secret symbol. It will stow away OneDrive from the Document Pilgrim.

7.   One more move toward be taken, pick More and you select Quit OneDrive. It will dispose of the OneDrive symbol from the notices segment.

For Windows 8.1.

8.   At the point when you access your PC start window, you will snap and hold the OneDrive symbol, and after then you will handpick Unfasten from Start.

9.   You can go to PC Settings, utilizing the PC Settings symbol toward the Beginning menu, you will handpicked Settings, and after then you handpicked Substitute PC settings.

10.   You can actually take a look at underneath the PC settings, handpicked OneDrive.

11.   At the point when you mind the Record Stockpiling tag, you will switch off the control at Save archives to the OneDrive through defaulting.

12.   Taking a gander at the Camera roll tag, you need to pick don't transfer photographs and afterward you break off the control at Auto transfer recordings to the OneDrive.

13.   Investigating the Sync settings tag, underneath Sync settings with the OneDrive, you break off the control at Sync settings on your PC.

14.   At the point when you view from the Meter associations tag, you can break off every one of the vital controls.

15.   For you to pelt OneDrive effectively from the Record Pilgrim, you want to get to the Document Adventurer and looking from the organizer list on the left, you will right-tap on the OneDrive and after then you click on Properties.

Taking a gander at the General tag, at the Properties, you will confuse the Secret symbol.

At the point when you check the Record tag, you need to tap on Unlink the PC and after then you Unlink account.

HOW TO UNINSTALLED ONEDRIVE

A few Windows naturally have OneDrive in them. The OneDrive application accompanies Windows 8.1 and Windows RT 8.1, you can't uninstall them from your PC, yet with respect to any semblance of Windows 7, Windows Vista, Windows XP, and different releases of Window 10 you can undoubtedly uninstall OneDrive from them. You can't uninstall OneDrive from Windows 10 cell Phone.

At the point when you effectively uninstalled OneDrive it will quit synchronizing right away, yet any document or information that you have in OneDrive can be realistic assuming you sign in to your record > OneDrive.com.

The most effective method to unlink for Windows 10.

1.   Simply click the Beginning menu, you type the Projects in the hunt box, and after then you click on Add or eliminate programs from the outcomes displayed to you.

2.   In the event that you look underneath the Applications and highlights, find and handpicked Microsoft OneDrive, and after then you click on Uninstall. At the point when you are affected for a regulator secret key, then, at that point, you will type the secret word or you convey approval.

Windows 7 or Windows Vista.

3.   Simply select the Beginning menu, taking a gander at the hunt box, you will type in Add Projects, and afterward, from the rundown of results displayed to you, you select Projects and Highlights.

4.   Select Microsoft OneDrive, and you click on Uninstall. At the point when you are affected for a regulator secret key, then, at that point, you will type the secret word or you convey approval.

Android gadgets.

5.   You simply go to Settings and pick Stockpiling/Memory.

6.   Just handpicked OneDrive and hit Uninstall.

iOS gadgets.

7.   You simply go to the Home Screen, tap, and clutch the OneDrive application symbol

8.   You simply tap X that shows in the upper left flank of the application symbol on your gadget.

macOS.

All you want to do here is to drag the OneDrive application to the Trash

THE BENEFIT OF MICROSOFT ONEDRIVE FOR BUSINESS

Microsoft OneDrive decidedly affects business. It promotion business through for sure. Under this sub-heading, we will let you know a portion of the significance of OneDrive concerning business. The following is the significance of OneDrive with business.

• It will help you in putting away and orchestrating your work documents in an extremely protected position in the capacity cloud that you can access whenever.

• It likewise helps you on the most proficient method to impart records or reports to your partner, so they can likewise go through or alter the substance of the documents. This course of sharing records or reports is exceptionally simple and special when contrasted with the most common way of fixing it to the email message.

• Microsoft OneDrive helps you in synchronizing records or reports put away in the capacity cloud to your PC or cell phone, this will assist you with opening your documents or archives on OneDrive disconnected absent a lot of pressure.

Notes: Microsoft embraces that all administrators store their business records on their OneDrive for Business purposes, it isn't their private OneDrive. Microsoft OneDrive for Business deals more prominent proficiency and organization/sharing elements intended for the workstation to be great.

HOW TO USE ONEDRIVE FOR SMALL SCALE BUSINESSES

We know that Microsoft OneDrive is vivacious yet this is simply to utilize capacity cloud platform in setting a norm for limited scope organizations, endeavors, and different things inside them. About most capacity cloud providers, when you take a gander at a significant number of the creative undertaking primary elements in OneDrive are generally possible for all membership types, which help the foundation while utilizing OneDrive in any perspective that benefits them. Assuming you notice, you will see that this sub-heading bargain more on the game plan and arrangement choices which gets more thoughts terms of limited scope organizations which need to include the utilization of OneDrive. As of now, the foundation can pick some other overseeing abilities required.

The Microsoft OneDrive has made it more straightforward and secure to reserve and open your documents from all of your gadgets. You can likewise work with others regardless of whether they are in or out of your affiliation and excuse the sharing of anything you wish. Microsoft OneDrive guides in safeguarding your work through creative encryption in the mean time the information is in shipment and very still in server farms. OneDrive can help to ensure that administrators keep your most requesting quiet submission guidelines by allowing them to pursue decisions where their information remains alive and giving a far reaching report of how that information has been exchanged and gotten to. Microsoft OneDrive connections you to your common documents in Microsoft 365, further developing association ability inside Microsoft 365 applications. On OneDrive on the web, work area, or portable, you can open all of your records incorporating the documents imparted to you from different groups, including documents from Microsoft Groups and SharePoint.

HOW TO GET STARTED WITH ONDRIVE FOR BUSINESS

OneDrive is exceptionally significant in any event, with regards to huge scope business, yet it is extremely difficult to carry out a strategy that limited scale organizations can acquire from it. By and large, limited scope organizations are dependably at a greater gamble of dropping documents which has blaming hardware in light of the fact that relatively few are with reinforcements and coordinated stockpiling. While utilizing OneDrive, your limited scale business will actually want to store every one of your documents for you securely, and it will simplify it for your administrators to reach out to it from their different frameworks.

To begin with OneDrive, you need to follow these means beneath:

1.   Step by step instructions to assess basic OneDrive data. All you want to do is to begin by changing the rudimentary OneDrive data reachable at the OneDrive assistance community. There will be a reaction to a few inquiries you wish to pose, even the experience of OneDrive and how it takes care of business.

2.   By setting up Microsoft Office 365 membership. You should set up a membership before you can utilize OneDrive, yet truth is that you are not compelled to purchase each application in Microsoft Office 365 suite.

3.   To Add OneDrive licenses. You will audit your different arrangement options in Analyze OneDrive plans, and after then you will add the licenses you need.

On the off chance that you have effectively done the assignment above, you are because of anticipating, position, and organize the OneDrive sync application and its applications. For it to be finished, you need to finish the accompanying three stages underneath:

1.   Plan to take on. While managing limited scope organizations, on the off chance that you intend to embrace different administrators it is consistently simpler as when you tell your administrators the best way to utilize OneDrive individual. Besides, concerning limited scope business clients generally don't esteem this step for new applications, and these can influence the application's advancement gravely.

2.   To introduce and orchestrate. The applications that are use to match up are consistently possible for macOS and Windows working frameworks which gives the administrators the experience to associate with their records without pressure. In uncommon cases limited scope organizations start by you downloading and introducing of sync application on your administrators' frameworks, after you are finished with that you can now imagine introducing OneDrive versatile application. Honestly, you have the OneDrive client on your frameworks. Particularly with gadgets utilizing Windows 10 working framework and that which is utilizing macOS with Microsoft Office 2016 or some other time we will have the OneDrive sync application.

3.   To deal with your OneDrive. In such countless limited scope organizations, overseeing OneDrive isn't consider vital. You can simply introduce the OneDrive application and design it minus any additional activity been finished on it. In a circumstance where you need to utilize a model construction of OneDrive or access constraints, which you can oversee them easily and numerous settings in the OneDrive administration center.

THE KEY ONEDRIVE STRUCTURES FOR SMALL SCALE BUSINESSES

For most distributed storage providers, the OneDrive doesn't offer enthusiastic designs to limited scope organizations have a place its breaking point, however it helps for the most part in the accessibility of a few current designs. This warrants the limited scale organizations with the capacity to involve current designs depending on the situation by their foundation.

These designs frame in this unit bargain on basic client nerves or careful understanding required, or give a cool capability that is just reachable in the OneDrive.

The OneDrive Records On-Request

The OneDrive Records On-Request improves the administrators to see, search, and furthermore speak with those documents which is been put away in OneDrive from the Record Pilgrim, and you didn't try to download each record to your framework. This specific person seems like across the board when view, for OneDrive and nearby records however consumed adequate room on your hard drive. Very much like it has been introduced to you in the image beneath illustratively, those records that poor person been download have a cloud symbol to show their status. In any case, for those documents that were downloaded, it will show a mark in green.

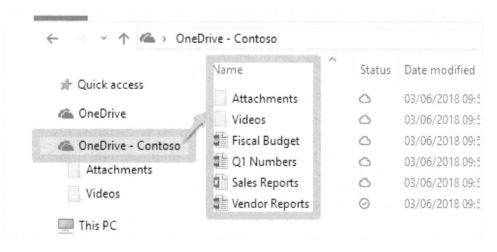

With defaulting, you can download any documents when you need to utilize those records. Also, on the off chance that you wish to open the records in any event, when you are not on the net how you will respond, is to make the document possible for you when you are disconnected. You should simply, perfectly click on the record and pick Generally keep on this gadget. Another choice is the point at which you really want some free space on your framework and you need to dispose of each and every duplicate of the record you download, perfectly click on the document and decide to Let loose space. The image beneath gives you a commonplace model appearance to you the right-click menu of the OneDrive documents on a Windows working framework.

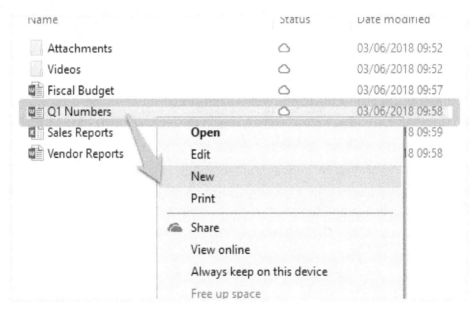

The modern connections

The Microsoft OneDrive acclimatizes with Microsoft Viewpoint to improve sharing of OneDrive documents showing just as an email connection with next to no type of pressure. This person specifically gives a notable sharing contribution however it has a bound together stockpiling add-on in OneDrive. Its grants generally your administrator which coordinate on a comparable document to stay away from fro and to sending of unique

70

releases in sends. You can likewise orchestrate record sharing consents directly from around the standpoint client.

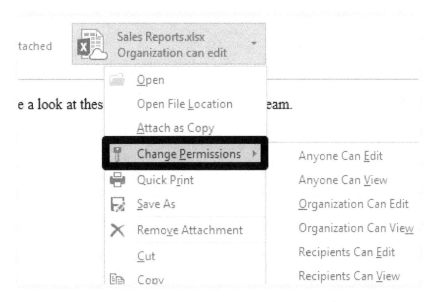

Instructions to reestablish documents

This component has by OneDrive enables you to reestablish any records that you have lost for around 30 days unique. For you to pick a superior chance to recuperate your document, OneDrive convey to you a histogram that assesses the action of the record for you to make a legitimate idea of the specific time you need to recuperate your records. From that point forward, simply click on the document history and select the ones you wish to reestablish and different shifts. The screen capture beneath is a run of the mill illustration of a record histogram.

Adding to what we have talked about, for the way that histogram assesses crafted by clients on document. This component can likewise be utilized to see the variation history of your records absent a lot of pressure.

The reuse canister.

The Microsoft OneDrive likewise has its own reuse container that is practically equivalent to the one which is possible on Windows work area. At the point when you erase any records it moves consequently to the reuse container and it will store it for a program period before it will be erased at last. For the record made for the everyday schedule, documents you have erased will be dispensed with for 93 days aside from you adjust the design.

The Realized Envelope Move.

This specific component upgrades the administrators to pick Windows-realized envelopes like Records, Work area, or pictures to mechanically adjust it to Microsoft OneDrive. This component can be added toward the starting OneDrive arrangement or after when you have designed it. The work done by this element award a change elective for those administrators looking to add known envelopes to their generally existing ones that are now synchronized.

ADOPTING ONEDRIVE FOR BUSINESS

Extricating from administrators is exceptionally fundamental concerning the general advancement of any new application. In a decent setting to have the outlook of expanding your interest in Onedrive and Office 365, there is a requirement for you to build the degree of commitment administrators have with them. On account of limited scope organizations, spurring administrator reception is extremely simple by presenting OneDrive during the time spent establishment.

In a circumstance where you tell your administrators the best way to share and save the report in Microsoft OneDrive is by all accounts a significant option on account of driving reception, for the way that you will be running Manual establishment for the primary time. The rudimentary idea for limited scope organizations utilizing OneDrive is the attainable quality of records and overt repetitiveness. At the point when you save a report in a manual stockpiling gadget you can undoubtedly lose it yet for those saved to OneDrive is extremely challenging to lose. All you really want to do is to have this discussion with your administrators, representing the applications on the most proficient method to utilize it, which could bring out benefit capable outcomes.

INSTALLING AND SETTING UP MICROSOFT ONEDRIVE FOR BUSINESSES

Under this, you can transfer, download, and help out your Microsoft OneDrive records from any net program, yet the OneDrive information begins from the Windows and Macintosh sync applications and the iOS and Android portable applications. With these clients and applications, saving records to Microsoft OneDrive and helping out them is extremely simpler than when you visit a site any time you need anything. Through this information, you can easily absorb OneDrive into your overall document correspondence inclusions.

There is likewise a requirement for you to introduce Microsoft OneDrive on a few supported gadgets. On account of limited scope organizations, the actual associations make the best insight. On account of different gadgets, the course of the establishment could be exceptionally simple very much like when you download an application from the play store. However, on account of others, there is a requirement for you to kill the old versions of Microsoft OneDrive. At this unit, you are to figure out the establishment and arrangement of Microsoft OneDrive on Android portable, iOS, Windows gadgets, and PC running macOS. There is no requirement for you to introduce on each platform relying upon the gadgets utilized in your affiliation.

MANAGING ONEDRIVE FOR BUSINESSES

Various limited scope organizations use Microsoft OneDrive without rotating a portion of the other options.

At the point when you need to add any principal gadget and sharing restrictions to OneDrive, you ought to utilize the OneDrive administrator place. For you to get to the new OneDrive administrator community, visit https://admin.onedrive.com. Then, at that point, you can limit individuals with whom your administrators can share documents, you can choose the gadgets your laborers can use to get to Microsoft OneDrive. This is only a brief of it, there are other explanative subtleties of it

CHAPTER 5

OTHER TASKS AND ICONS ON ONEDRIVE

There are several icons which is found on Microsoft OneDrive which makes it to perform multiple function. Under this chapter am going to explained in details how you can go around using various icons/functions found on Microsoft OneDrive.

FUNCTION OF EMBED BUTTON ON ONEDRIVE

In the event that you have a site or blog, it's speedy and simple to implant photographs, Office reports, and different records from OneDrive. You might in fact alter how implanted Succeed exercise manuals appear to others.

Everybody on the web stores valuable family photographs, significant work records, PDFs, music, and all in the middle of between on something many refer to as the "cloud".By having our stuff up on the web saves us the difficulty of stacking up our documents on our little USB sticks and opens up our cell phone and PC's memory.Putting away records on the cloud additionally works on our efficiency at function as we can get to significant work documents from anyplace on the planet.

It assists us with decreasing those feared email strings and extended periods of time looking for documents on our laptops. One of the main players in the distributed storage and the record sharing business sector is Microsoft's own, OneDrive.

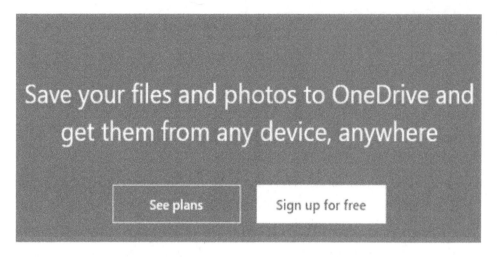

OneDrive is a distributed storage administration by Microsoft that permits clients to store every one of their records reports, pictures, recordings, music, and other rich media on the cloud. It permits clients to get to their documents from any gadget - telephones, tablets, or PCs.

Any progressions made by you will be refreshed on the entirety of your gadgets, making sharing and altering records, a consistent encounter. OneDrive additionally gives disconnected admittance to records, and that implies you can continuously get to your most significant documents consistently.

Understand more: Instructions to Implant Behance Motivations Into Your files/documents.

USE BIT DOCUMENTS TO EMBED ONEDRIVE FILES

The mystery ingredient to Spot is its capacity to make records like no other archive supervisor out there. Bit assists you with making records representing things to come that are dynamic and considerably more than plain-exhausting message.Aside from permitting various clients to team up on archives, Bit additionally permits clients to share any kind of rich media like YouTube recordings, SoundCloud Playlists, install Google Sheets, Docs, and Slides, One Drive Succeed Bookkeeping sheets, GIFs, Tweets, Cloud documents, Pinterest sheets, and so forth. Fundamentally, anything on the web with a connection can be shared and Spot will naturally transform it into visual substance.

WHY WE EMBED ONEDRIVE IN A BIT DOCUMENTS

1. No interruptions!

We frequently share our cloud records with our companions over email. Then we attempt to make sense of what's going on with the record in the accompanying messages, and in practically no time you're suffocating in an ocean of inquiries and replies!

At the point when you have your significant substance spread around various gadgets and apparatuses, your efficiency generally assumes the lower priority. It turns into very much simple to lose all sense of direction in an ocean of program tabs, and break that work process!

Perusing many organizers, looking in your disordered and greatly populated inbox, looking through your cloud records, and so on, all turn out to be a pursuit mission that is difficult to break.

2. Lucidity of work

Here and there you believe that something other than an email should make sense of what's going on with a specific record. You want setting, data, and text to cause your companions and partners to comprehend what the OneDrive record that you just shared is about and how they should manage it.

Implanting an OneDrive record inside a Cycle report furnishes you with that truly necessary space to examine, give ideas and criticism, and team up really without individuals being lost and feeling confounded and permits you to impart that substance related to different types of computerized content.

3. Cooperate productively

It's essential to smooth out your applications and diminish the work process wreck that we make for ourselves by teaming up inside every individual device or through email and visit.

It's vital to have the option to bring all of your cloud records, information, content, and in particular, individuals, under a solitary virtual rooftop.

Where every one of your reports, accounting sheets, promoting, and deals security, inner wikis, and information and coincide without the requirement for different outsider specialized apparatuses.

HOW TO EMBED ONEDRIVE IN BIT DOCUMENT

With Bit, you can reorder any OneDrive cloud weblink-Succeed Accounting sheets, PowerPoint, Word records, PDFs, and so forth. On a clear line of a Piece record and hit enter. No more managing chaotic iFrame/insert code!

We should perceive how you can implant a Succeed Calculation sheet put away in OneDrive onto a Cycle report in 4 simple tasks!

1. Open up your OneDrive Excel Spreadsheet and snap the more button on the upper right corner.

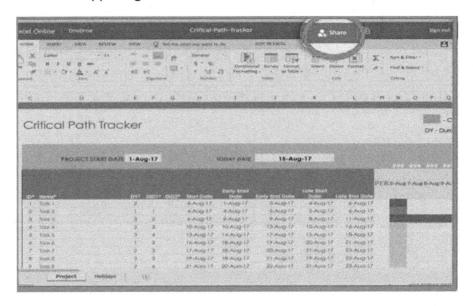

2. Make and duplicate your shareable connection.

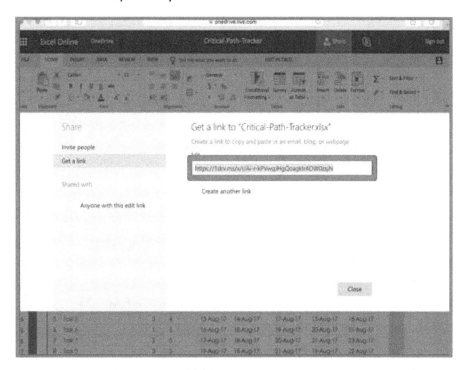

3. Go to Bit.ai and glue the OneDrive Excel Spreadsheet weblink on a clear line and hit enter.

4. Digit will consequently bring the OneDrive Excel Spreadsheet and show it like this.

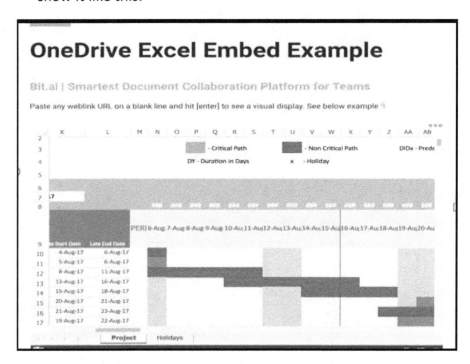

UNDERSTANDING ONEDRIVE APPLICATION FOR DESKTOP

Microsoft OneDrive is a free document stockpiling and record sharing help accessible to any Microsoft account client. Microsoft OneDrive gives one terabyte of capacity to free. You consequently approach on the off chance that you make a free Microsoft email record, or you can make a free Microsoft account utilizing any email address like Gmail or Yippee!.

OneDrive records and envelopes can either be gotten to through an internet browser or by means of a work area application. They can likewise be gotten to through a portable application on a cell phone. This module will zero in on work area use, yet remember that comparable usefulness is accessible on the web and portable applications.

HOW TO CREATE FOLDERS IN ONEDRIVE

After you download the OneDrive work area application, you might have previously been approached to sign in. Whenever you are endorsed in, you can see OneDrive as an organizer in your Windows Document Pilgrim.

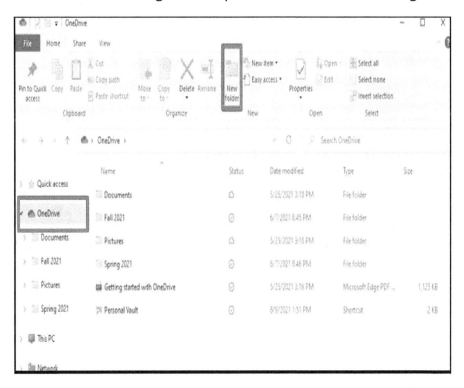

In the Record Pioneer, you can make OneDrive envelopes very much like you would some other organizer on your PC. To make another envelope, you can all things considered:

• click the New envelope button on the lace, or

• right snap some place in the OneDrive envelope sheet and select New>Folder.

ONEDRIVE ON A Macintosh.

Microsoft OneDrive is accessible for download on a Macintosh and will work in much the same way. You will simply utilize the Locater rather than the

Windows Pioneer to explore through your OneDrive envelopes and documents.

Transferring and Putting away Records in OneDrive.

To save a file in OneDrive, open the document and snap File>Save As. Then select the OneDrive envelope or subfolder where you need to save it.

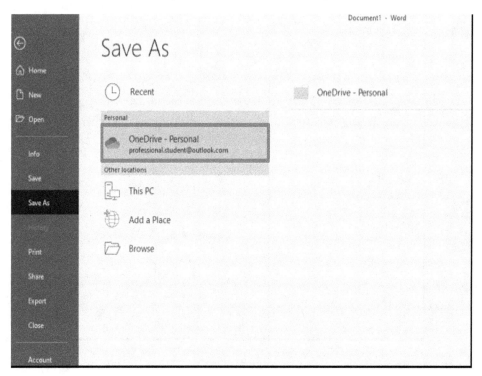

Syncing Files to the Cloud

The OneDrive envelope in the Record Pioneer has a section called Status. The symbols in this section give you subtleties on the situation with matching up the record or envelope in the distributed storage.

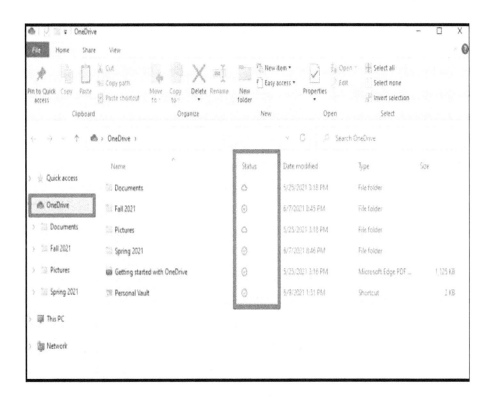

HOW TO SHARE FILES IN ONEDRIVE

To share a record from the OneDrive envelope in the Document Pioneer, right snap on the record and select Offer. You might see numerous choices to share. Provided that this is true, select the one with the OneDrive blue cloud symbol close to it. Note that you can share the two records and envelopes utilizing this strategy. Assuming that you share an envelope, you are sharing admittance to all records at present in that organizer and that might be added to that envelope later on.

When you click on Offer with the blue cloud symbol, you will see choices to enter email addresses alongside a message to send it through that exchange box, or you can duplicate the connection to share another way, (for example, by email or talk). Select the choices you need on your connection by clicking Anybody with the connection can alter.

• Permit altering. You can uncheck this case in the event that you don't believe anybody with the connection should have the option to alter the document.

• Set termination date. In the event that you set a lapse date, the connection will just work until the date you set.

• Set secret key. In the event that you set a secret word, the client will be provoked to enter a secret key before they can get to the record. You should send the secret phrase independently to anybody you might want to give access.

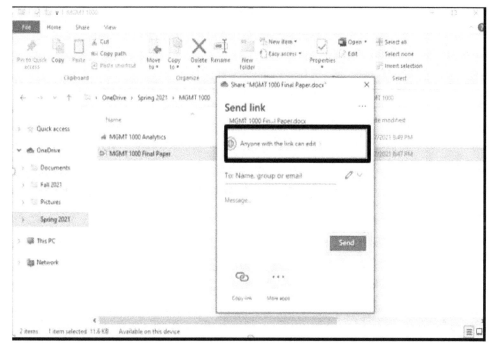

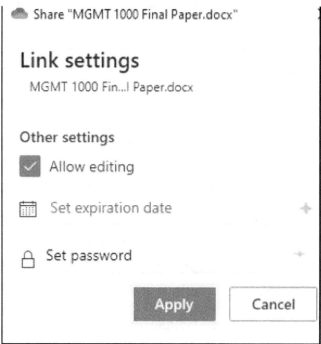

In your email, you can likewise share OneDrive records as a connection as opposed to connection. A discourse box will seem when you select an

OneDrive record as the document you might want to join to the email. Then, at that point, you can choose either Offer connection or Append as duplicate.

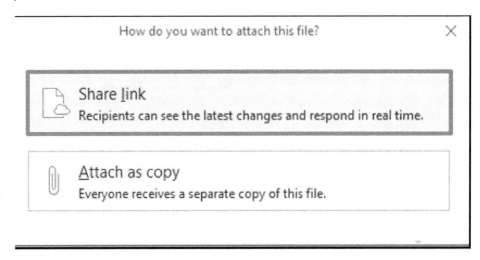

BETTER WAY TO SYNC FILES IN MICROSOFT ONEDRIVE

In the event that you meet a few OneDrive images not permitted to match up, or the OneDrive status symbol not refreshing, which in some cases implies that your OneDrive not synchronizing accurately. Or on the other hand you would rather not get familiar with these complex OneDrive images, it's strongly prescribed to attempt the free cloud reinforcement administration - CBackup, which permits you to reinforcement or sync records to OneDrive with practically no document size or move speed constraint and you can adjust documents without a hitch.

To simplify everything, you can uninstall the OneDrive work area application first, then attempt CBackup to match up documents to OneDrive naturally. The beneath steps are inclined to adjust documents to OneDrive naturally.

1. If it's not too much trouble, introduce the CBackup work area application, make a free CBackup account then, at that point, sign in.

Secure Download

2. Select the Stockpiling tab, then, at that point, pick OneDrive, and hit Approve Now.

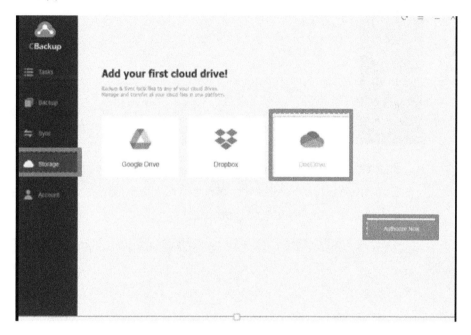

3. Tap Sync > Sync PC to Public Cloud in this way.

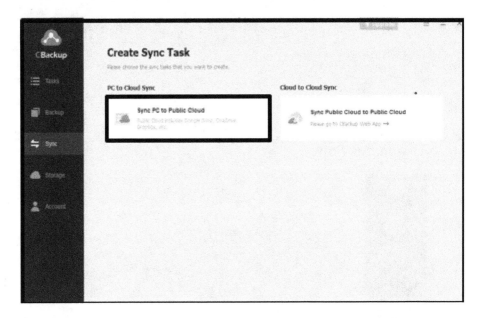

4. Pick the PC documents in the Source segment, and select an OneDrive envelope as the objective. Hit Settings > Scheduler to empower OneDrive programmed sync.

5. Raise a ruckus around town Sync button to match up records to OneDrive naturally.

CHAPTER 6

CHANLLENGE OF MISSING ICON IN ONEDRIVE

The OneDrive is a record facilitating administration and synchronization administration presented by Microsoft. It is a significant device in Windows, particularly for the people who need to adjust records and envelopes. It likewise empowers you to move records to the distributed storage.

In Windows 10, the OneDrive is constantly shown on the right of the Taskbar. The symbol is the doorway to get to the OneDrive. In any case, sadly, the OneDrive symbol now and again may vanish from the taskbar, causing clients to experience issues in getting to OneDrive. What's more, OneDrive symbol additionally vanishes in the Document Pioneer.

OneDrive symbol missing Windows 10 is a serious issue to be sure. Thus, this post will direct you on the best way to fix the issue Windows 10 OneDrive missing from Taskbar and Document Traveler. The arrangements will be shown individually.

FIXING ONEDRIVE ICON MISSING FROM TASKBAR

In any case, we will exhibit how to fix the issue OneDrive symbol missing from the warning region. Assuming that your OneDrive symbol vanishes from the Taskbar, attempt these arrangements.

SOLUTION 1. Ensuring OneDrive Symbol Isn't Appearing in Secret Region

In the event that you have a great deal of symbols on the Taskbar or the Framework Plate, a few symbols will be covered up. So assuming you find the OneDrive has missed from the Taskbar, check whether it is covered up first and foremost.

Then, at that point, simply click the vertical bolt like symbol the Taskbar and check whether the OneDrive symbol is here.

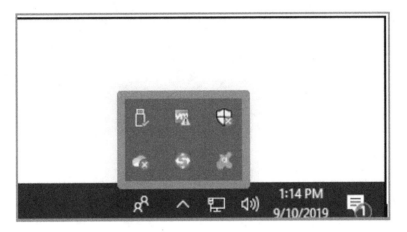

Solution 2. Empower OneDrive Symbol in Taskbar

On the off chance that the OneDrive isn't concealed in the Taskbar, you really want the second technique to settle the issue OneDrive symbol missing. In this arrangement, you can check whether you have empowered the OneDrive symbol in Taskbar. If not, you want to do that.

Presently, we will tell you the best way to empower OneDrive symbol in Taskbar.

Step 1: Open Taskbar settings
1.   Right-click on the Taskbar.

2.   You will see a setting menu and pick Taskbar settings to proceed.

Step 2: Enable OneDrive icon in Taskbar

1. In the popup windows, if it's not too much trouble, look down to the Warning region and pick Select which symbols show up on the taskbar to proceed

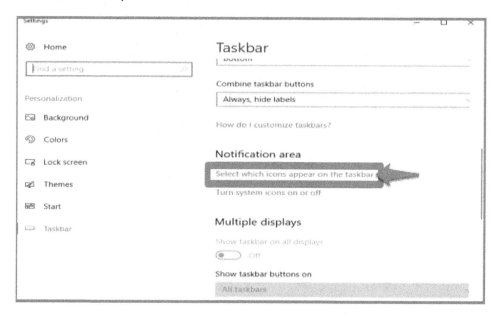

2. Figure out the Microsoft OneDrive, and afterward change the flip change to On.

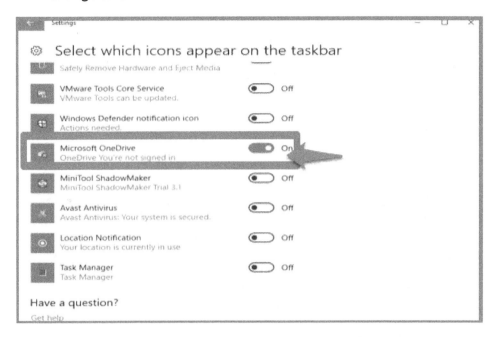

From that point forward, you can leave the Taskbar settings window and check whether the issue OneDrive symbol missing from Taskbar is tackled.

Solution 3. Reset OneDrive

In the event that the above arrangements don't work to OneDrive cloud symbol missing, you can have a go at following arrangement. In this arrangement, take a stab at resetting OneDrive.

Presently, we will tell you the best way to reset OneDrive with the bit by bit guide.

Step 1: Open Run program

1. Press Windows key and R key together to open Run exchange.

2. Reorder the accompanying code to the container and snap alright to proceed.

%localappdata%\Microsoft\OneDrive\onedrive.exe

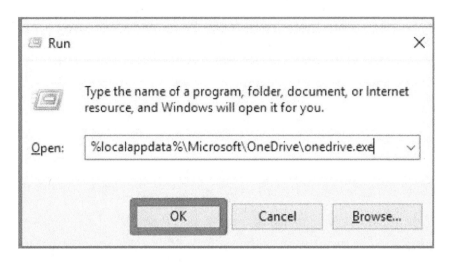

Step 2: Begin to reset OneDrive

1. Then, at that point, a window of Microsoft OneDrive arrangement up will show up. The OneDrive will be introduced for first use.

2. Then, at that point, you are expected to sign in OneDrive.

3. From that point onward, you will see the OneDrive symbol is accessible in the Taskbar. Right-click it and pick Settings.

3. In the spring up window, if it's not too much trouble, go to the Settings tab and check the choice Beginning OneDrive naturally when I sign in to Windows. Then, at that point, click alright to proceed.

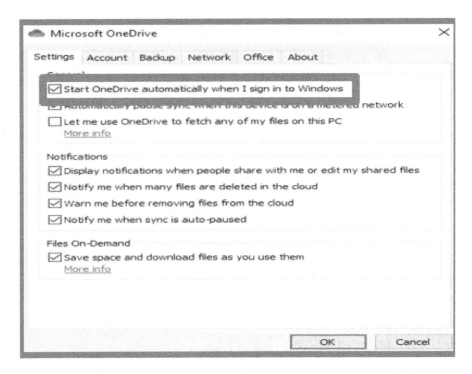

From that point forward, you can see the issue OneDrive symbol not showing is addressed and it is in the Taskbar. Then, at that point, it will be sent off consequently when you sign in Windows. Likewise, this arrangement additionally can be utilized to fix the issue OneDrive symbol missing from Document Pilgrim. For additional answers for OneDrive symbol not appearing in Document Wayfarer, we will show them in the accompanying segment

Solution 4. Check Policy Settings

To fix the issue Windows 10 OneDrive missing, we will exhibit you the fourth arrangement. You can take a stab at really looking at the Strategy settings.

Presently, we will show you the instructional exercises.

Step 1: Open Neighborhood Gathering Strategy Supervisor window

1.   Press Windows key and R key together to open Run exchange.

2.   In the crate, input gpedit.msc in the case and snap alright to proceed.

Step 2: Actually look at strategy settings

1. In the Neighborhood Group Strategy Manager windows, explore to the OneDrive envelope as per the accompanying way.

PC Design > Managerial Layouts > Windows Parts > OneDrive

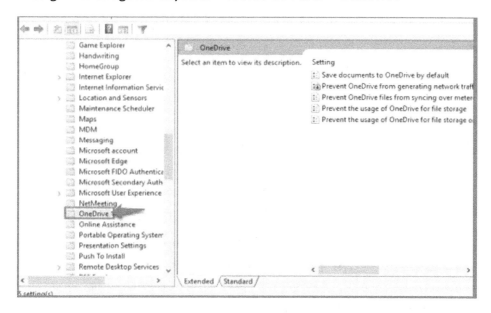

2. On the right board, pick Forestall the utilization of OneDrive for document capacity and double tap it.

3. In the spring up window, pick Not Designed, and afterward click Apply and alright to affirm the changes.

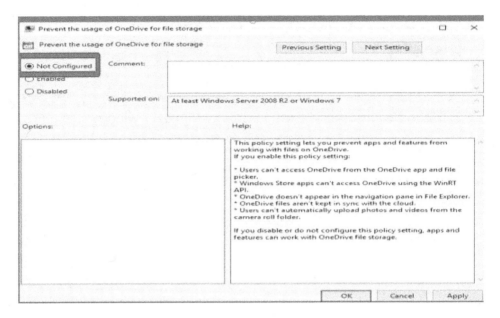

At the point when you have completed all means, you can reboot your PC and check the issue OneDrive symbol missing from Taskbar is settled. Additionally, this strategy likewise can be utilized to fix the issue OneDrive symbol missing Windows 10 from Record Voyager. What's more, we won't make reference to this technique in the How to Fix OneDrive Symbol Missing from Document Adventurer area once more.

Solution 5. Set up OneDrive from Scratch

On the off chance that none of the arrangements is successful, you might have to reinstall OneDrive. What's more, presently, we will tell you the best way to reinstall the OneDrive with the bit by bit guide.

Step 1: Open Order Line Window

1.   Type Order Brief in the hunt box and pick the best-matched one.

2.   Right-click it to pick Run as head.

Step 2: Type the orders

In the order line window, type the orders individually and hit Enter to proceed.

For Windows 10 32-cycle:

%SystemRoot%\System32\OneDriveSetup.exe/uninstall

%SystemRoot%\System32\OneDriveSetup.exe/introduce

For Windows 64-cycle:

%SystemRoot%\SysWOW64\OneDriveSetup.exe/uninstall

%SystemRoot%\SysWOW64\OneDriveSetup.exe/introduce

FIXING ONEDRIVE ICON MISSING FROM FILE EXPLORER

As we have referenced in the above area, the OneDrive symbol might vanish from Taskbar and Document Pioneer. We have acquainted how with fix OneDrive symbol missing from the notice region. Also, in this part, we will tell the best way to settle OneDrive symbol missing in Document Voyager.

Solution 1. Remove All OneDrive Entries

To fix OneDrive symbol missing in Record Pilgrim, you can take a stab at eliminating all OneDrive passages in Library. We will show you the itemized instructional exercises in the accompanying segment.

Note: Rolling out certain improvements in the Vault is something unsafe, so satisfy back up the PC ahead of time in order to keep away from certain mishaps. Furthermore, this arrangement just works for Windows 7/8. In the event that you are a Windows 10 proprietor, attempt different arrangements.

Step 1: Open Library Proofreader window

1.   Press Windows key and R key together to open Run discourse.

2.   Input regedit in the container and snap alright to proceed.

Step 2: Eliminate OneDrive passages

1. In the Vault Proofreader window, go to Alter tab and pick Find... to proceed.

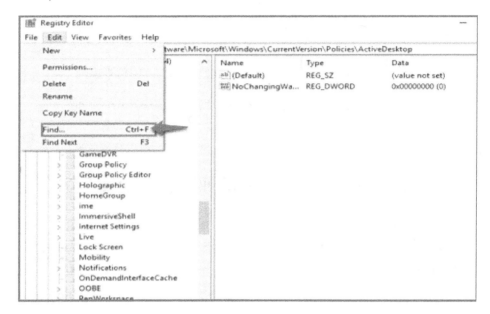

2. In the case, input onedrive and check all Gander at Then click See as Close to proceed.

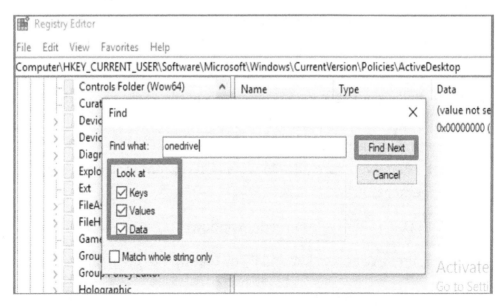

3. Then eliminate the OneDrive section by clicking Erase. They are a few OneDrive sections, so find and eliminate them individually with similar advances.

At the point when you have completed all means, reboot your PC to check whether the OneDrive symbol missing issue is addressed.

Solution 2. Modify the Registry

Presently, we will show you one more answer for Windows 10 OneDrive symbol missing. In this arrangement, you can adjust the Vault.

Step 1: Open Library Supervisor window

1.   Press Windows key and R key together to open Run discourse.

2.   Input regedit in the crate and snap alright to proceed.

Step 2: Change the Library

1. In the Library Manager window, kindly explore to the accompanying organizer. On the off chance that you don't have the OneDrive key, you ought to make another one.

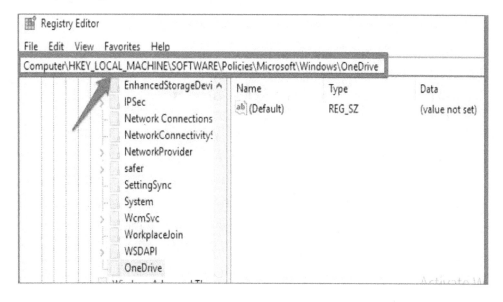

2. On the right board, right-click the DisableFileSyncNGSC string and pick Adjust to proceed. In the event that it is missing, right-click the right board and pick New and DWORD(32-bit) worth to make another one.

3. Then, at that point, change its worth information to 0. Then, at that point, click alright to proceed.

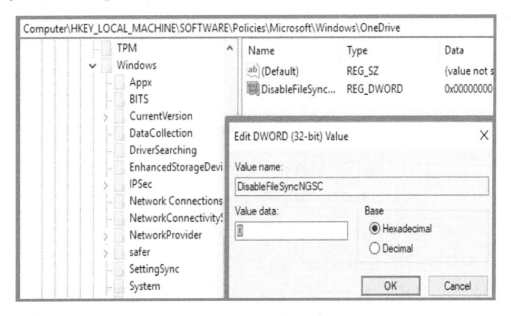

At the point when you have completed every one of the means, you can reboot your PC to produce results and check whether the issue OneDrive cloud symbol missing is addressed.

Solution 3. Use Other File Sync Software

Assuming you have attempts every one of the above arrangements, however the issue OneDrive symbol missing still happens. You can decide to attempt one more piece of record sync programming. Other than the OneDrive symbol missing issue, you may likewise experience a few different issues during the utilization cycle, for example, OneDrive sync not working or OneDrive sync forthcoming. Thus, to decrease the difficulties, you can attempt other record sync programming. Thus, MiniTool ShadowMaker is a decent decision. It is a piece of expert synchronization and reinforcement programming. It empowers you to adjust documents to at least two areas to protect information.

Aside from that, MiniTool ShadowMaker likewise assists you with matching up huge documents fast and simple. In the event that you have an enormous number of documents to be synchronized, you can decide to clone the entire hard drive to another. Indeed, you can decide to clone the operating system from HDD to SSD. Presently, we will tell you the best way to match up records to one more hard drive with MiniTool ShadowMaker.

Step 1: Send off MiniTool ShadowMaker

1.   Download MiniTool ShadowMaker and introduce it.

2.   Send off it.

3.   Click Keep Preliminary.

Step 2: Select Sync Source

1.   In the wake of entering its fundamental connection point, go to the Sync page.

2.   Click the SOURCE module to pick document sync source. Click alright to proceed.

Step 3: Select sync objective

1.   Click the Objective module to pick sync objective.

2.   The following are five ways accessible including Director, Libraries, PC, Organization and Shared envelopes. Choose where you need to save the synchronized records and snap alright. Picking an outer hard drive is suggested.

Step 4: Begin to Adjust Records

1.   In the wake of choosing the sync records and objective, click Sync Now to match up documents.

2.   Or on the other hand you can decide to click Sync Later and restart this undertaking in the Oversee page.

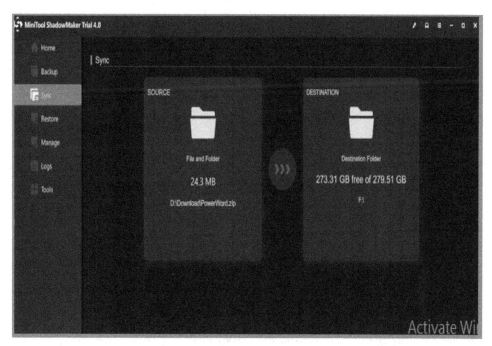

At the point when you have completed all means, you have effectively synchronized records to another hard drive. With this record sync programming, don't stress over what to do while experiencing OneDrive symbol missing from Taskbar or Document Pilgrim once more.

CONCLUSION

With what we have made sense of that far ought to have the option to deal with numerous issues concerning Microsoft OneDrive. You ought to have the option to know how to set up Microsoft OneDrive on unique working frameworks. At this point you ought to be aware to share records, reports from your PC to your Microsoft OneDrive record. Subsequent to going through the slide you will know how to match up, transfer and deal with your documents with no type of pressure by any means. It is accepted that with the guide of this slide you can do various bundles on OneDrive. This little documentation makes sense of exhaustively how for get more space on your Microsoft OneDrive record. This slide likewise goes further in giving a point by point clarification of how to deal with your OneDrive record. It likewise illuminates how to disengage OneDrive from your PC. There are more things you will acquire from these slides even regarding business.

At last, in the event that you have quietly gone through this slide, you will likewise know how to deal with the business utilizing Microsoft OneDrive. You will actually want to open the OneDrive archive both on the web and disconnected. This documentation goes with a ton of illustrative models, which will direct you in finishing any job with practically no type of pressure. It will be of much assistance to the individuals who need the information on Microsoft OneDrive at the rudimentary level. By following the illustrative model given to you in this documentation you can oversee Microsoft OneDrive effortlessly. It is accepted that as you go through this slide you ought to have the option to comprehend the fundamental idea of OneDrive.

www.ingramcontent.com/pod-product-compliance
Lightning Source LLC
LaVergne TN
LVHW081531050326
832903LV00025B/1730